What's the Point of Christmas?

J . J O H N

A LION BOOK

Contents

Countdown to Christmas

Fun and frustration; peace and panic; excitement and exhaustion; feasting and fattening; spending and spending and spending.

But then Christmas arrives. Frustrations fall away. The panic is over. We are left with wonder and joy. Children's faces light up, excitement is in the air.

Yet because of the rush we find it hard just to stop and think.

After all, why do we follow all these customs? Where on earth did they all come from? Isn't it funny that just because we are born into a world of customs, we grow up accepting them?

What's it all about?

St Nicholas–
the first Santa

We tell children to hang up their Christmas stockings on Christmas Eve and ('as long as you go to bed early') the next morning they find their stockings filled with toys and sweets.

Do you think children ever wonder how Santa Claus gets down the chimney without getting stuck? And how is it he doesn't dirty the sitting room? But then, maybe he sweeps up before he leaves!

We see Santa Claus as a jolly old gentleman with white whiskers, rosy cheeks, dressed in a fur-trimmed coat and hood, driving his reindeer team through the skies—maybe the Superman idea came from Santa!

The original Santa Claus was St Nicholas, the Bishop of Myra in Asia in the fourth century. He was one of the most overworked saints ever.

One story about him is that because the bishop was a shy man, he liked to give money anonymously to the needy. So, one day, he climbed the roof of a house and dropped a purse of money down the chimney of a family of needy girls. The purse landed in the stockings which the girls had hung up by the fire to dry.

In memory of him it became customary to give gifts on the eve of St Nicholas Day, 6 December.

The first Christmas presents were brought by wise men to a child called Jesus. Today, too, we exchange presents to express our love for each other.

In some countries this tradition has continued. In others this was transferred to 25 December, our Christmas Day.

A Christmas
built of cards

Christmas cards can be a pleasure and a pain. It can be a real pleasure to keep in touch with old friends around the country and beyond. If we can get down to writing them, we can keep these old friends up to date with our news.

But what a pain deciding when the mailing list should stop! On many occasions my decision about who should receive a greeting card was made on who sent me one the year before!

Isn't it difficult when you have sent out all your cards and then a neighbour drops a card round on 24 December when you don't have any left? But wait a minute, why do we send these cards anyway? Where did they originate?

The first Christmas card was made in 1843 by Sir Henry Cole, founder of the Victoria and Albert Museum, London. The card was sent to Mr John Horsley and was titled 'Brimming Cheer'. It pictured a family celebrating Christmas and giving gifts of clothing and food to the poor.

Nowadays millions of cards are sent all over the world, with a variety of messages from peace and goodwill to partying; from snowmen to the Saviour of the world.

The prince and the bishop

Christmas is hardly complete without a tree. It brightens your home and brings joy to children everywhere.

When eventually it's put into a plastic bucket and filled with soil, there's an agonizing hour (or more, depending on experience) to get the tree to stand upright. Only then can you sit back in your armchair with a smile to congratulate yourself on this great success.

Until, that is, you realize you didn't buy a sprayed tree . . . and, oh no! . . . its needles have covered the carpet! Then it's on with the coloured lights and electric flex . . . only to find that the lights aren't working again!

What's the tree for anyway? The Christmas tree goes back to the eighth century to a missionary from England called St Boniface.

Boniface went to Germany to teach people the Christian faith. There, one December, he encountered a group of people standing beneath an oak tree ready to sacrifice a child to please their god.

Boniface immediately rescued the child and chopped the oak tree down. At its foot was a small fir tree. He cut the small fir tree and gave it to the people as a symbol of life. He called it the tree of the Christ-child.

The story continues when Martin Luther, the famous German church leader, cut a fir tree and took it home in the December of 1540.

The evergreen tree reminded him that life continued through the winter, when most of nature appeared to have died. He attached a number of small candles to illuminate the tree to express that Christ was welcome in his home.

In the middle of the nineteenth century, the Christmas tree was introduced into England by Queen Victoria's husband, the German-born Prince Albert. Its popularity increased from then on as part of the celebration of Christmas.

An evergreen tree has been adopted as a symbol of continuing life.

Silent night! holy night!
All is calm, all is bright
Round the virgin and her child:
Holy infant, so gentle and mild,
Sleep in heavenly peace;
Sleep in heavenly peace!

Silent night! holy night!
Shepherds quail at the sight,
Glory streams from heaven afar:
Heavenly hosts sing, 'Alleluia,
Christ the Saviour is born,
Christ the Saviour is born.'

Silent night! holy night!
Son of God, love's pure light:
Radiant beams your holy face
With the dawn of saving grace,
Jesus, Lord, at your birth,
Jesus, Lord, at your birth.

J.F. Young

A Christmas carol

One picture we have of traditional Christmas is
of snow-lined streets with carol singers gathered
under a lantern.

But the carol, too, is largely a Victorian invention.
And the picture comes from the ever-popular
Charles Dickens and not some medieval custom.

True, the origin of some of our carols goes back
hundreds of years. But what they meant by a *carole*
was a form of dance rather than a Christmas hymn!
So, where's the connection?

Well, we dance when we celebrate, so alongside
more sophisticated Christmas music there grew up
a tradition of simple popular songs suitable for
celebrating the birth of Jesus.

The famous *Stille Nacht* (Silent Night) is one of
these simple songs, composed in an evening!

The story goes that on Christmas Eve 1818 the organ in the village church of St Nicholas-in-Obendorf was found to be faulty. The culprit was a hungry mouse which had eaten through the bellows.

The curate Joseph Mohr, in some desperation, brought a poem to the organist to see if he could arrange it for a choir led by a guitar. He could and he did. And when the carol was duly performed (with great success) it was quickly taken up by other churches in Germany.

From the late middle ages until almost 200 years ago carols were somewhat neglected. But in the last century there was renewed interest in the traditions of the past.

There was also an enthusiasm to sing, so old Latin hymns were translated and long-forgotten books dusted and scoured for material. Hymn singing became central to church life. Dr Henry John

In this painting of St Wencelas Square, Prague, singers celebrate the greatest present ever given —God's gift to us of his Son.

Gauntlett, who composed the music for *Once in Royal David's City*, claimed to have written 10,000 hymn tunes.

Traditional carols were rediscovered, new carols were written, and music from many sources was pressed into service, although not always with the approval of the composer.

Mendelssohn complained when one of his tunes was used for *Hark! the Herald Angels Sing*—it was originally part of a work to celebrate the four hundredth anniversary of printing and

Mendelssohn thought it too 'soldier-like and buxom' for use as a carol.

Nothing evokes memories of childhood more vividly than the sound of a favourite Christmas carol. A warm glow comes over us . . .

But the words recall far more than presents, laughter and fun. They retell the story of how God became man. And there's nothing childish in that. It is the most amazing thing that has ever happened.

The twelve days of turkey

Christmas food is arriving . . . and keeps arriving:
lunch time, tea time, supper time! Then it's served
up on Boxing Day, at lunch time and supper time
and rehashed for the next day. Let's hope there's
none left for the day after! But why turkey?

Yes, why the turkey, a Mr William Connor asks:
'the turkey has practically no taste except a dry
fibrous flavour reminiscent of a mixture of warmed-
up plaster of Paris and horsehair'!

Oh, it's not that bad, Mr Connor. It's special.
That's why we have it at Christmas.

The turkey was introduced into Europe in the
sixteenth century by Sebastian Cabot, an officer
on a return journey from the New World which had
just been discovered, which is where the birds came
from. They were called turkeys because merchants
from Turkey popularized them.

The idea of a mid-winter feast has a long history.
The Romans and the less civilized folk of northern
Europe celebrated the shortest day of the year: the
feasting helped them to forget the long nights and
cheered them with the thought that summer days
were ahead.

The Roman festival lasted from 17 December until
the Kalends of January which was the Roman New

Year when business accounts were settled. Kalends gives us our word 'calendar'.

Like Christmas today, a holiday was declared, presents were exchanged and houses were decorated with evergreens—holly, ivy and mistletoe — to represent continuing life and luck. Bawdy plays were performed, with men dressed in women's clothing—the original winter pantomime!

Whatever we might think of them, these customs and traditions and many others continue. But it can be a bit of a surprise to discover that they don't actually originate from Jesus Christ, the main person in *CHRIST*-mas.

Now that's not to say they don't have any value, but in probing into the real meaning of Christmas we find that they are really only the wrapping paper, the box in which Jesus Christ, the true meaning of Christmas, lies.

Why do we decorate our homes at Christmas? What is the real meaning behind the glitter and tinsel?

Putting the record straight

Before going further, let's put the record straight about the date of our celebrations.

The early church did not know the exact date of Jesus' birth, neither was there any annual celebration of the event.

The Bible tells us that 'while shepherds watched their flocks by night', Jesus was born. So we know it wasn't in December: the shepherds and the sheep would have frozen in the Palestinian winter!

The first evidence for the celebration of Jesus Christ's birth on 25 December is found in a Roman document dated AD336. The date was chosen as a Christian take-over of the Roman festival celebrating the unconquerable *Sun*. The apparently dying Sun began to increase its sunlight on 25 December.

And when an early Pope sent St Augustine to convert the barbaric Anglo-Saxon tribes in northern Europe he urged his missionary to fit Christian celebrations around local traditions. Here, too, Augustine found mid-winter revelries lasting twelve days. Our word Yule-tide is derived from the name of an Anglo-Saxon god and again the celebrations concerned the rebirth of the sun. But Augustine told them of the true God become man. So, as in Rome, instead of worshipping the

Mary and Joseph went from the town of Nazareth in Galilee to the town of Bethlehem in Judea. Mary was pregnant, and while they were in Bethlehem, the time came for her to have her baby.

Sun, Christians began to use the festival to celebrate the birthday of Jesus Christ and to worship instead the unconquerable *Son*.

21

Let's also put the record straight about the real meaning of Christmas. Christmas is about the coming of Jesus Christ into the world. Jesus Christ came into the world to rescue us from the mess we were in.

That's quite a statement, but we only need to look around today to see that we have got problems in the world:

● Socially we are in one of the most violent periods in our history. It is estimated that some 25 million people have died in war *since* World War II alone and that the total this century exceeds 100 million.

● Domestically, family life is in crisis everywhere. In the West, one out of three marriages break up. Two children a week die at the hands of their own parents. Juvenile crime is on the increase . . .

● Individually, many people have a growing feeling of insignificance. Mother Teresa has said: 'The greatest disease today is not starvation but loneliness.' Loneliness is the feeling of not mattering to anyone, of being worthless, of being isolated even when surrounded with people.

A way in a manger

In Luke's Gospel we read that an angel called
Gabriel came from heaven to a virgin called Mary.
As you can imagine she was rather troubled! But
the angel said to her:

> 'Do not be afraid, Mary, you have
> found favour with God. You will be
> with child and give birth to a son, and
> you are to give him the name Jesus. He
> will be great and will be called the Son
> of the Most High. The Lord God will
> give him the throne of his father David,
> and he will reign over the house of Jacob
> for ever; his kingdom will never end.'

This was the Annunciation, the announcement of
what God was going to do.

Mary was asked to bear a child not of human
descent but born of God; born to rescue us from
death and darkness and to enable us to take our
place in the family of God.

Mary was engaged to be married to Joseph, so you
can imagine how Joseph felt when he discovered
that his fiancée was pregnant. He knew that he
had nothing to do with it! How could he possibly
marry a girl who was expecting a baby by someone
else? Yet he couldn't back out without other people

23

finding out why. Then Mary's reputation would be ruined.

While Joseph considered what to do, an angel told him the true nature of the situation in a dream.

> 'Joseph, do not be afraid to take Mary
> home as your wife, because what is
> conceived in her is from the Holy Spirit.
> She will give birth to a Son, and you are
> to give him the name Jesus.'

Meanwhile, in Rome, Caesar Augustus, Emperor and 'master book-keeper', issued an order for a census of the world.

On the fringe of his empire in a little village called Nazareth, where Mary and Joseph lived, soldiers nailed up an order for all citizens to register in the towns of their family origin. Joseph, because of his family line, had to register in King David's town of Bethlehem. So Mary and Joseph set out to go there.

Five hundred years earlier the prophet Micah had prophesied concerning that little village:

> 'But you Bethlehem, though you are
> small, out of you will come for me,
> one who will be ruler over Israel, whose
> origins are from of old, from ancient
> times.'

They arrived in Bethlehem and Joseph looked for a place to stay. As he entered the city, Joseph must have been desperate to find lodgings for Mary: the child was due any time. Joseph went from inn to

inn only to find each one crowded. He must have been anxious and close to panic.

The only shelter to be found was a stable, where shepherds drove their sheep in times of stormy weather.

The inn is the gathering place of public opinion, the focal point of the world's moods. But the stable is a place for the outcasts, the ignored, the forgotten.

There, Mary and Joseph went at last for shelter. There, in the loneliness of a cold, windswept stable, Jesus was born.

> 'Today in the town of David, a Saviour
> has been born to you. He is Christ the
> Lord.'

No one could ever again think of God as being remote, or 'somewhere up there . . . ' When Mary gave birth to Jesus she held in her arms the Guest who was also the Host of the world.

Wrapped in linen strips, his first bed was a straw-filled manger, the feeding trough of the animals.

God wrapped in swaddling clothes?

God lying in a manger?

No one would have ever suspected that God coming
to earth would ever be so helpless. And that is
precisely why so many fail to find him.

Just imagine . . . if you had the whole world
at your fingertips, if you were able to choose
where and how you were to have your first baby,
what kind of place would you choose? A first-rate
hospital . . . ? Comfortable and warm surround-
ings . . . ?

Yet God, who could have chosen anywhere, chose
the lowliest place on earth.

From the moment of his birth, Jesus identified with
poverty and pain.

In the bleak mid-winter
Frosty wind made moan,
Earth stood hard as iron,
Water like a stone;
Snow had fallen, snow on snow,
Snow on snow,
In the bleak mid-winter
Long ago.

Our God, heaven cannot hold him,
Nor earth sustain;
Heaven and earth shall flee away
When he comes to reign;
In the bleak mid-winter
A stable-place sufficed
The Lord God Almighty,
Jesus Christ.

What can I give him,
Poor as I am?
If I were a shepherd,
I would bring a lamb,
If I were a wise man,
I would do my part;
Yet what I can I give him—
Give my heart.

C.G. Rossetti

In dark streets shining

Suppose you found in your attic an old oil-painting, covered over with the grime of centuries.

Imagine your excitement as you cleared away the dust to reveal a name such as Rembrandt or Holbein! Then, after painstaking cleaning and care, the long-lost original could once more be hung to reveal the artistry of its creator.

God becoming man in Jesus is also an act of restoration. The world is his creation; we are made in his image. And yet the rebellion of centuries has marred this image. We are no longer what God intended.

And so Jesus came to begin the cleaning process. In his own character he showed us what God is like, what we are intended to be, and what we might become.

In his life he healed the sick and banished spiritual forces of evil, repainting the world so it reflected the original intention.

People who listened to the teachings of Jesus said, 'No man ever spoke like this man.' His personality and character matched the remarkable nature of his teaching.

Jesus had a great sense of humour and laughed, yet was known as a man of sorrows.

He played with children and took babies in his arms, yet the most hard and cruel men withered beneath his glare.

He was known as a man of compassion and love, yet people quaked before his anger.

He was a man of courage and strength, yet his whole life spoke of humility. He combined patience with power.

He taught us how we should live our lives, how we should deal with our anxieties, worries and needs. He revealed to us the perfect path to take.

Jesus talked about normal things, weddings, funerals, children playing, money lost, a neighbour who had run out of food, unexpected guests. He spoke about the flowers of the fields, the birds of the air, bread, fish, clothes, water. Jesus dealt with life.

He cared for others whatever their need. He accepted others whatever their background or race. He touched the untouchable—the lepers in society. He treated women with courtesy and encouraged their own sense of self-worth in a culture that subordinated them to men.

Jesus recognized the worth of each person he met. He had compassion when they were hurting. He touched those suffering from fever, leprosy, epilepsy. He gave mobility to paraplegics, sight to the blind, hearing to the deaf, speech to the mute. He restored withered limbs, diseased organs, degenerating spines. He cured haemorrhages and skin sores.

In this 'little town of Bethlehem' Jesus became man and lived among us.

He did all this to restore creation to the one who made it. And he wanted to make it clear to us what God is like. He does care. He is concerned about the evil in the world. In the person of Jesus, God got involved with the battle against evil, and showed that he doesn't just stand by while we suffer.

And it is from Jesus we learn that no person stands higher than when he or she stoops to serve. His self-sacrifice has motivated many throughout history to serve others.

Mother Teresa of Calcutta and the Missionaries of Charity are examples of those trying to follow Jesus' life and teaching.

Mother Teresa said:

'I have found the paradox that if I love until
it hurts, then there is no hurt, but only more
love. As I held and fed the morsel of life that
was an aborted baby, as I held the hand of a
man dying from cancer and felt his trust and
gratitude, I could see, feel and touch God's
love which has existed from the beginning.'

But how can we talk of God's *love* when there
is still so much suffering? If God became man in
Jesus why hasn't the world been put right once
and for all? His miracles of healing provided only a
temporary clean-up in one small part of the world.

Is it simply that his life has inspired others, and we
must take up the battle where he left off?

Or is there something more?

31

O little town of Bethlehem,
How still we see thee lie!
Above thy deep and dreamless sleep
The silent stars go by:
Yet in thy dark streets shineth
The everlasting light;
The hopes and fears of all the years
Are met in thee tonight.

How silently, how silently,
The wondrous gift is given!
So God imparts to human hearts
The blessings of his heaven.
No ear may hear his coming;
But in this world of sin,
Where meek souls will receive him,
Still the dear Christ enters in.

O holy Child of Bethlehem,
Descend to us, we pray;
Cast out our sin and enter in;
Be born in us today.
We hear the Christmas angels
The great glad tidings tell;
O come to us, abide with us,
Our Lord Emmanuel.

P. Brooks

On the cards

Despite our peace greetings to each other at Christmas, the world is still in conflict and chaos.

Many attempts at peace have been short-lived. Thousands of peace treaties have been signed over the years.

On 25 December 1914, during the First World War, while the Germans and the Allied armies faced each other in France, someone began singing the carol 'Silent Night, Holy Night'. A hush fell over the battlefield.

Soldiers on both sides laid down their arms, climbed out of their trenches and met together. Men who had spent weeks trying to kill each other now embraced, sang and exchanged souvenirs and cigarettes. Even a football match was organized . . .

And then, on 26 December, they went back to their trenches once again to kill each other.

As we approach Christmas, we find ourselves surrounded by decorations, lights and carols promoting joy and festivity. Yet it is also the time of year when suicides, family quarrels, depression and drunkenness reach a peak.

Peace in our time?

Peace to whom? There will not be peace in the

Jesus came to bring light and hope into a world that does not acknowledge him.

world until the main problem in the world is sorted out. And the heart of the human problem is the problem of the human heart. An ancient Jewish writer understood this when he wrote:

> 'Who can understand the human heart?
> There is nothing else so deceitful.'

We were created in God's likeness to live in the world and to enjoy an intimate relationship with him. Because God is love we were not forced into this friendship. We were given the free will to choose: to accept or to reject God.

But right from the start, and then down through

the years of history, we have turned away. We have turned from our Creator, choosing our way rather than his.

We have shut God out of our lives.

And because of this breakdown of communication, something or someone was needed to heal the divide—someone to stand between God and us, a go-between, someone who shared and understood our humanity yet who was untainted by our sinfulness.

But because no prophet or priest, seer or saint could fulfil that role, God himself became man in the person of his Son, Jesus.

This is the meaning of Christmas: the babe at Bethlehem. It was the coming among us of God himself, to restore the world we have messed up.

Joy to the world! the Lord is come!
Let earth receive her King!
Let every heart prepare him room,
And heaven and nature sing.

Joy to the earth! the Saviour reigns!
Let men their songs employ!
While fields and floods, rocks,
Hills, and plains
Repeat the sounding joy.

No more let sins and sorrows grow,
Nor thorns infest the ground;
He comes to make his blessings flow
Far as the curse is found.

He rules the world with truth and grace,
And makes the nations prove
The glories of his righteousness,
And wonders of his love.

Isaac Watts

Back to Bethlehem

Many people had been waiting for the arrival of Jesus the Saviour. But at his birth only two sorts of people came to welcome him, some shepherds and some wise men, the simple and the learned, those who knew that they knew nothing and those who knew that they did not know everything.

The shepherds were tending their flock on the hills nearby when angels announced to them the birth of Jesus Christ. The shepherds said to one another:

> 'Let's go to Bethlehem and see this
> thing that has happened, which the
> Lord has told us about.'

The wise men were astronomers from the east. Following a star they came to Jerusalem and they asked:

> 'Where is the one who has been born
> King of the Jews? We saw his star in the
> east and have come to worship him.'

When Herod, King of Israel, heard this he was worried. Having called together the chief priests, he discovered that the Christ was to be born in Bethlehem.

He met with the wise men and sent them to Bethlehem with instructions to report where the

new King had been born. He told them that his desire was to worship him too.

The wise men were warned in a dream not to tell Herod the whereabouts of the baby. Herod had said that he wanted to worship him, but his actions proved that he really meant 'If this is the King, I must kill him, because he is a threat to me.'

> 'Herod gave orders to kill all the boys
> in Bethlehem and its vicinity who were
> two years old and under.'

Herod will for ever be the model of those who make enquiries about Jesus Christ. His motives were wrong and therefore he misused the knowledge that he received.

What people ask about Jesus Christ is never as important as the reason why they ask it. Herod pretended he wanted to bring gifts to honour and worship the King. But the only thing he wanted to bring him was death.

38

Wise men travelled from afar to worship the new King.

But the wise men did bring gifts:

● They gave Jesus gold, the best they had, to honour his Kingship.

● They gave Jesus frankincense, a symbol of prayer, to show their desire to communicate with God.

● They gave Jesus myrrh, a symbol of death, to acknowledge what he had come to earth to do.

Peace with God

Imagine the whole of your life projected on to a screen in front of you. It reveals everything you have done, everything you have said and everything you have ever thought.

How would you feel seeing it on your own?

How would you feel seeing it in the presence of everybody involved in the film as well?

Some of it would be great. But all of it?

Can any of us say that we have led a perfect life? Have we never become bitter and resentful with anyone? Have we never stolen anything—not even a person's reputation? Have we never coveted our neighbour's possessions . . . ?

No. We have all failed in some way. We have all sinned.

Because we have sinned it is as if we have an overdraft of sin. As we all have an overdraft of sin we cannot help each other. Being good may prevent our overdraft from getting worse but it doesn't clear it. We still remain in debt, guilty and cut off from God.

Only someone in credit, someone without sin, can deal with our overdraft.

Jesus Christ is the only one who can clear it. He

is the only one who is perfect, sinless. To clear our overdraft, he had to die the death due to human sin. This was the 'cheque', signed when he died on the cross. In this way he bought our forgiveness.

It is only when God deals with sin that forgiveness can be real, because we cannot live with God while we are guilty. Nothing sinful can exist in his presence.

We were made to live a life of friendship with him. But we have cut ourselves off from his presence—unless our guilt, our sinfulness, can be taken away.

An anonymous poet summed it up in these words:

'If our greatest need had been information,
God would have sent us an educator.

If our greatest need had been money,
God would have sent us an economist.

If our greatest need had been technology,
God would have sent us a scientist.

If our greatest need had been pleasure,
God would have sent us an entertainer.

But our greatest need was forgiveness,
So God sent us a Saviour.'

With the death of Jesus Christ, peace with God is made possible.

Feelings of hostility with ourselves, with others and with God can be dealt with. When our overdraft of sin is cleared we can experience the joy of being in

41

God's family. We can call God 'Our Father'.

But it didn't stop there. Jesus not only dealt with sin, he conquered death. He died, but three days later he rose from the dead.

Jesus Christ is alive today. He continues to live within every person who receives him, by giving us his Spirit.

Peace and goodwill to all?

That peace can only come when we have peace with God.

The angels brought a message of great joy. In Bethlehem a Saviour was born, a Saviour who would bring us peace with God.

As with gladness men of old
Did the guiding star behold,
As with joy they hailed its light,
Leading onward, gleaming bright:
So, most gracious Lord, may we
Evermore be led to thee.

As with joyful steps they sped,
Saviour, to thy lowly bed,
There to bend the knee before
Thee whom heaven and earth adore:
So may we with willing feet
Ever seek thy mercy seat.

As they offered gifts most rare
At thy cradle rude and bare;
So may we with holy joy,
Pure, and free from sin's alloy,
All our costliest treasures bring,
Christ, to thee, our heavenly King.

Holy Jesus, every day
Keep us in the narrow way;
And when earthly things are past,
Bring our ransomed souls at last
Where they need no star to guide,
Where no clouds thy glory hide.

W.C. Dix

All we want for Christmas

If we accept that we have sinned, we can come to Jesus Christ the Saviour and be forgiven.

C.S. Lewis wrote, 'Forgiveness from Jesus Christ is like a tape-recording of your life wiped completely clean.'

That is fantastic!

We can then enter into a personal relationship with Jesus by receiving his Spirit.

This is the gift of Christmas. But, like all our Christmas gifts, he needs to be received.

Will you receive him this Christmas?

Will you, like the wise men:

—Bring myrrh by looking to Jesus' death for forgiveness?
—Bring frankincense by entering into a relationship with him?
—Bring gold by giving your life, the best you have got?

If you want to receive him, pray this prayer by saying these words:

Thank you, Jesus, that you left heaven and came into this world as a child. Thank you for all that I can learn from your life. Thank you that you died for my sins. I know that I have sinned and I am sorry. Please forgive me. Come into my life by your Spirit. Help me from this moment to show that I belong to you by following you. Amen.

This is the beginning of a relationship with Jesus Christ: the very best basis for enjoying a Merry Christmas!

We often feel Christmas is really 'for the children'. But the gift of Jesus Christ is available freely for all to receive.